RANJOT SINGH CHAHAL

Productivity Pro

Practical Strategies and Tips for Success

AF517311

Rana Books

First published by Rana Books (UK, INDIA) 2023

Copyright © 2023 by Ranjot Singh Chahal

All rights reserved. No part of this publication may be reproduced, stored or transmitted in any form or by any means, electronic, mechanical, photocopying, recording, scanning, or otherwise without written permission from the publisher. It is illegal to copy this book, post it to a website, or distribute it by any other means without permission.

First edition

Contents

Chapter 1: Setting SMART Goals

In the journey of success, the initial step of any plan is to set specific, measurable, achievable, realistic, and time-bound (SMART) goals. The process of setting goals helps you pick where you aim to go in life. By clearly understanding what you want to achieve, you are less likely to wander off the track and waste time on sidelines. Goals provide a sense of direction and purpose in our lives.

1.1 Defining Specific Goals

One of the key elements of setting SMART goals is ensuring that they are specific. A specific goal clearly outlines what you want to achieve and provides a roadmap for how to get there. By defining your goals with precision you increase the likelihood of success and can effectively measure progress.

Example 1: Non-Specific Goal
"I want to get in shape."

This goal is too broad and lacks specificity. It leaves room for interpretation and does not provide a clear direction. To make it specific you need to define what "getting in shape" means to you personally.

Example 2: Specific Goal
"I want to lose 10 pounds and improve my cardiovascular endurance by running three miles without stopping within three months."

This goal is specific as it clearly outlines the desired outcome and the specific actions required to achieve it. It provides a tangible target to work towards.

1.2 Ensuring Goals are Measurable

Measuring progress towards your goals is essential for staying motivated and tracking your success. By establishing measurable goals you can objectively assess your progress and make adjustments if necessary.

Example 3: Non-Measurable Goal
"I want to improve my cooking skills."

While this goal implies improvement it fails to provide a way to measure that improvement. To make it measurable you need to identify specific indicators or milestones that can be tracked.

Example 4: Measurable Goal
"I want to learn five new recipes and successfully cook each one at least three times within six months."

This goal is measurable because it includes specific activities and a time frame in which progress can be tracked. It provides concrete evidence to determine whether the goal has been achieved or not.

1.3 Working towards Achievable Goals

Setting achievable goals means ensuring that they are realistic and attainable. It's important to consider your available resources skills and limitations when defining your goals.

Example 5: Non-Achievable Goal
"I want to become a professional golfer within a year despite never having played golf before."

While it's admirable to aspire to become a professional golfer this goal may be too ambitious and unrealistic. It is essential to set goals that are within your reach based on your current abilities and circumstances.

Example 6: Achievable Goal
"I want to improve my golf handicap by five strokes over the next six months by taking regular lessons and practicing for at least three hours a week."

This goal is achievable as it acknowledges the need for skill development and sets a realistic target for improvement. It considers the time and effort required to attain the desired outcome.

1.4 Setting Realistic Goals

Setting realistic goals is closely related to setting achievable goals. Realistic goals take into account external factors such as time resources and competing priorities.

Example 7: Non-Realistic Goal
"I want to write a bestselling novel within a month even though I have a full-time job and family responsibilities."

While it's wonderful to have aspirations of writing a bestselling novel this goal may not be realistic given the writer's current time constraints. It's important to set goals that align with your commitments and available resources.

Example 8: Realistic Goal
"I want to write a draft of a novel within one year by dedicating at least one hour daily to writing."

This goal is realistic as it considers the writer's current time constraints and sets achievable expectations. It allows for consistent progress while managing other responsibilities.

1.5 Time-Bound Goals

Setting a specific time frame for achieving your goals provides a sense of urgency and helps you manage your progress effectively. Time-bound goals keep you focused and prevent procrastination.

Example 9: Non-Time-Bound Goal
"I want to learn a new language."

While learning a new language is a valuable goal it lacks a clear time frame. Without a deadline it's easy to delay taking action or lose motivation.

Example 10: Time-Bound Goal

"I want to achieve conversational fluency in Spanish within nine months by dedicating at least 30 minutes every day for study and practice."

This goal is time-bound because it establishes a deadline for achieving conversational fluency. It provides a sense of urgency and allows for proper planning and progress tracking.

In conclusion setting SMART goals is a powerful tool for effective goal setting and accomplishment. By making goals specific measurable achievable realistic and time-bound you provide yourself with a roadmap for success. Use these principles to define your goals and increase your chances of achieving them. Remember to review and adjust your goals periodically to ensure they remain relevant and aligned with your aspirations.

Chapter 2: Prioritizing Tasks

Prioritizing tasks is a crucial skill for effective time management and productivity. It involves evaluating the importance and urgency of various responsibilities to allocate time and resources efficiently. By setting clear priorities, individuals can ensure that they focus on high-impact activities that align with their goals. Prioritization helps prevent feeling overwhelmed and ensures that essential tasks are completed first. It often involves creating to-do lists, using tools like the Eisenhower Matrix, and considering deadlines, consequences, and personal preferences. Effective prioritization not only enhances productivity but also reduces stress and boosts overall performance. It's a skill applicable to both personal and professional life, helping individuals achieve their objectives systematically.

2.1 Differentiate between Urgent and Important Tasks:

When it comes to prioritizing tasks it's crucial to understand the difference between urgent and important tasks. Urgent tasks require immediate attention and have a pressing deadline while important tasks are tasks that have a significant impact on achieving your goals or fulfilling your responsibilities. Understanding this distinction allows you to prioritize effectively and avoid getting overwhelmed by a sense of urgency.

For example imagine you have a project deadline at the end of the week (urgent) and a meeting with your team to discuss long-term strategy (important). Both tasks are valuable but it's important to recognize that the project deadline requires immediate attention due to its urgency while the meeting holds long-term importance for the success of the team.

2.2 Using the Eisenhower Matrix:

One effective method for prioritizing tasks is the Eisenhower Matrix also known as the Urgent-Important Matrix. It helps categorize tasks based on their urgency and importance. The matrix has four quadrants:

1. Quadrant 1: Urgent and Important - These are tasks that require immediate attention and are critical to achieving your goals. Examples include meeting deadlines handling emergencies or addressing urgent client requests.

2. Quadrant 2: Important but Not Urgent - These are tasks that have a significant impact on your long-term goals but don't have an immediate deadline. Examples include strategic planning skill development relationship building and self-care activities.

3. Quadrant 3: Urgent but Not Important - These tasks demand immediate attention but have minimal impact on your long-term goals. Examples include phone calls unimportant meetings and some emails that don't require immediate action.

4. Quadrant 4: Not Urgent and Not Important - These tasks are neither urgent nor important and can be considered distractions or time-wasters. Examples include scrolling through social media unproductive conversations or excessive web browsing.

The goal of the Eisenhower Matrix is to focus your attention on Quadrants 1 and 2 as these are where the most valuable and impactful tasks lie. Quadrant 3 tasks should be minimized or delegated and Quadrant 4 tasks should be eliminated or greatly limited.

Using this matrix you can prioritize tasks effectively by focusing on what truly matters and avoid getting caught up in non-essential or low-value activities.

2.3 Pareto Principle: The 80/20 Rule:

Another useful concept for prioritizing tasks is the Pareto Principle also known as the 80/20 rule. This principle suggests that roughly 80% of your results come from 20% of your efforts. In other words a small portion of your tasks creates the majority of your outcomes.

By applying the Pareto Principle you can identify the most impactful tasks and prioritize them first maximizing your productivity and efficiency. This approach helps ensure that you're dedicating your time and energy to tasks that have a significant impact on your goals or responsibilities.

For example let's say you're an entrepreneur running an e-commerce business. Applying the Pareto Principle you may discover that 80% of your revenue comes from 20% of your products. By prioritizing the promotion optimization and development of this 20% of high-value products you can drive significant growth and profitability.

2.4 Assessing the Consequences of Delaying Tasks:

When prioritizing tasks it's essential to consider the consequences of postponing or delaying each task. Some tasks have immediate consequences if not addressed on time while others may have more long-term consequences.

For example paying a bill before the due date prevents late fees and potential service interruptions while delaying it could result in financial penalties or negative credit impacts. On the other hand delaying a less time-sensitive task like organizing your workspace may not have immediate consequences but could lead to decreased efficiency or increased stress over time.

2.5 Time Blocking:

Time blocking involves allocating specific blocks of time in your schedule to focus on particular tasks or categories of tasks. This technique helps you allocate dedicated, uninterrupted time for your most important and often challenging tasks. By structuring your day this way, you can improve productivity and ensure that important tasks receive the attention they deserve.

2.6 Delegate and Outsource:

Recognize that you don't have to do everything yourself. Delegating tasks to team members or outsourcing certain responsibilities can free up your time for higher-priority tasks. It's important to trust and empower others to handle tasks that are less critical to your role.

2.7 Regularly Review and Adjust Priorities:

Priorities can change, so it's crucial to regularly review and adjust your task list. What was urgent and important yesterday may not hold the same priority today. Stay flexible and adaptable to shifting circumstances and new information.

2.8 Practice the Two-Minute Rule:

If a task takes less than two minutes to complete, do it immediately. This rule helps you quickly address small tasks and prevents them from piling up and becoming a source of distraction or stress.

2.9 Maintain a Task List or Planner:

Keeping a task list or using a digital planner can be immensely helpful. Write down your tasks, deadlines, and priorities to keep them organized and easily accessible. Tools like to-do lists, calendar apps, or project management software can assist in managing your tasks efficiently.

2.10 Consider Your Energy Levels:

Recognize that your energy levels fluctuate throughout the day. Try to tackle your most important and challenging tasks when your energy is at its peak. Save routine or less critical tasks for times when your energy naturally dips.

2.11 Say No When Necessary:

Learning to say no to tasks or commitments that don't align

with your goals or priorities is a skill that can help you maintain focus on what truly matters.

By incorporating these additional strategies into your task prioritization process, you can further enhance your ability to manage your time effectively and achieve your goals efficiently.

In summary prioritizing tasks effectively involves differentiating between urgent and important tasks using tools like the Eisenhower Matrix and the Pareto Principle and assessing the consequences of delaying tasks. By understanding these concepts and applying them to your daily activities you can focus on tasks that truly matter maximize productivity and achieve your goals more efficiently.

Chapter 3: Effective Time Management

Effective time management is the art of maximizing productivity and achieving goals within a set timeframe. It involves setting clear objectives, breaking them down into manageable tasks, and allocating time wisely. By prioritizing tasks and eliminating distractions, individuals can make the most of their available hours. Time management often includes using tools like calendars, planners, or digital apps to schedule activities and stay organized. It's a valuable skill for balancing work, personal life, and leisure activities, leading to reduced stress and improved work-life harmony. Mastering time management ensures that individuals can meet deadlines, increase efficiency, and make the most of every precious moment.

3.1 Identify Time Wasters and Eliminate or Minimize Them

One of the fundamental steps to effective time management is identifying and eliminating or minimizing time wasters. Time wasters are activities or habits that consume a significant amount of time without contributing to your productivity and goals. By reducing or eliminating these time wasters you can free up more time for meaningful and important tasks.

Some common time wasters include excessive social media usage unnecessary meetings procrastination multitasking and disorganized workspaces. Let's take a closer look at each of them:

Excessive social media usage: Social media platforms can be addictive and spending too much time scrolling through feeds watching videos or participating in online discussions can easily eat up a significant portion of your day. To overcome this time waster you can set specific time limits for social media usage use website blockers to avoid distractions or allocate dedicated time for social media during your breaks.

Unnecessary meetings: Meetings can be a huge drain on time especially when they lack clear objectives or have too many participants. To minimize this time waster ensure that meetings have a clear agenda limit their duration and only invite those individuals who are necessary for the discussion. Additionally consider alternatives such as email updates phone calls or virtual meetings to save time.

Procrastination: Procrastination occurs when we delay tasks or choose to do less important activities instead of prioritizing our important tasks. This can be a major time waster as it often leads to rushing tasks at the last minute or missing deadlines. To overcome procrastination start by breaking tasks into smaller manageable steps create a schedule or to-do list and use techniques such as the Pomodoro Technique (discussed later in this chapter) to keep focused.

Multitasking: Contrary to popular belief multitasking is actually counterproductive and can lead to decreased efficiency and accuracy. When we try to juggle multiple tasks at once our focus and concentration suffer resulting in lower quality work and wasted time. Instead focus on one task at a time and allocate dedicated time for each task which allows you to complete them more efficiently and effectively.

Disorganized workspaces: Having a disorganized workspace can lead to wasted time searching for documents tools or supplies when you need them. Take some time to declutter your workspace organize your files digitally or physically and create systems to ensure easy access to the resources you need. This will help save time and increase productivity in the long run.

By identifying these time wasters and taking steps to minimize or eliminate them you can significantly improve your time management skills and make more efficient use of your available time.

3.2 Implementing Time Blocking Techniques

Time blocking is a popular time management technique that involves scheduling specific blocks of time for different tasks or activities. It helps you allocate dedicated time for important tasks enhances focus and ensures the completion of tasks within the set time frame. Here's how you can implement time blocking effectively:

Prioritize tasks: Start by identifying your most important and high-priority tasks. These are the tasks that have the greatest impact on your goals and require your immediate attention. By identifying your priorities you can allocate adequate time for them in your schedule.

Break down tasks: Next break down your tasks into smaller manageable chunks. This makes them more approachable and helps you allocate appropriate time for each subtask. Ensure that your time blocks are realistic and consider the complexity and time required for each task.

Allocate specific time blocks: Once you have your tasks broken down allocate dedicated time blocks for each task or category of tasks. For example you can allocate a two-hour block in the morning for important project work followed by a one-hour block for emails and communication. Be sure to include breaks between time blocks to rest and recharge.

Be flexible but disciplined: While time blocking provides structure to your schedule it's important to remain flexible when needed. Unexpected events or emergencies may arise and you might need to adjust your time blocks accordingly. However it's important to be disciplined and stick to your scheduled time blocks as much as possible to avoid unnecessary disruptions.

Use digital tools: Several digital tools and apps can help you implement time blocking effectively. Calendar apps like Google Calendar and productivity apps like Todoist or Trello allow you to create time blocks set reminders and track your progress. Experiment with different tools and find the one that suits your needs best.

By implementing time blocking techniques you can better

manage your time stay focused on important tasks and ensure greater productivity.

3.3 Breaking Tasks into Manageable Chunks

Breaking tasks into manageable chunks is a strategy that helps make complex or overwhelming tasks more approachable. It involves dividing larger tasks into smaller more manageable parts which allows you to tackle them more effectively. Breaking tasks into manageable chunks has several benefits:

Increased focus: When faced with a large task it's easy to become overwhelmed and lose focus. Breaking it down into smaller chunks helps you concentrate on one aspect at a time preventing cognitive overload and improving your ability to stay focused.

Clear milestones: Breaking tasks into smaller parts provides clear milestones that can give you a sense of progress and accomplishment. Completing each chunk gives you a sense of achievement motivating you to move forward and increasing your overall productivity.

Better time allocation: By breaking tasks into smaller chunks you can allocate appropriate time blocks for each subtask. This allows you to have a more accurate estimate of the time required to complete the entire task and helps you manage your time more effectively.

Reduced procrastination: Overcoming procrastination can be challenging especially when faced with daunting tasks. However breaking tasks into manageable chunks makes them less intimidating reducing the tendency to procrastinate. Each chunk becomes more manageable and less overwhelming making it easier to start and make progress.

To break tasks into manageable chunks follow these steps:

Identify the main task: Start by identifying the main task or project that needs to be completed. This could be a work-related project a personal goal or any other significant task.

Analyze the task: Next analyze the main task and determine the different components or subtasks it consists of. Consider what needs to be done and in what order. If necessary create a task breakdown structure or a mind map to visualize the subtasks and their relationships.

Break it down: Once you have analyzed the task break it down into smaller manageable chunks. Each chunk should be relatively independent and achievable within a reasonable time frame. Write down these subtasks and consider their order of completion.

Allocate time: Decide how much time you will allocate for each subtask. Consider the complexity and time required for each chunk and schedule them in your calendar or time-blocking system accordingly.

Monitor progress: As you complete each subtask mark it as complete and track your progress. Celebrate small wins to stay motivated and focused on the overall task.

By breaking tasks into manageable chunks you can overcome feelings of overwhelm improve focus and increase your productivity and efficiency.

3.4 Utilizing Pomodoro Technique

The Pomodoro Technique is a time management method developed by Francesco Cirillo in the late 1980s. It helps you break your work into focused intervals called "Pomodoros followed by short breaks. This technique aims to enhance your concentration productivity and overall work quality. Here's how to implement the Pomodoro Technique:

Set a timer: Start by setting a timer for a specific duration typically 25 minutes known as a "Pomodoro." This duration can be adjusted according to your preference and the nature of the task.

Work intensely: Once the timer begins work on a specific task with full focus and concentration until the Pomodoro is complete. Avoid any distractions or interruptions during this time.

Take a short break: When the Pomodoro ends take a short break of around 5 minutes. Use this time to rest stretch or do something enjoyable to recharge yourself. Avoid engaging in tasks related to your work during this break.

Repeat the cycle: After the short break start another Pomodoro and continue with your work. Repeat this cycle of focused work followed by short breaks until you reach a predetermined number of Pomodoros typically four and then take a longer break of 15 to 30 minutes.

Benefits of the Pomodoro Technique:

Enhances focus and concentration: By working in focused intervals the Pomodoro Technique helps you eliminate distractions and increase your concentration on the task at hand. This improved focus leads to higher quality work and greater productivity.

Prevents burnout: Regular breaks during the Pomodoro Technique prevent mental fatigue and burnout. They allow you to recharge avoid overwhelm and maintain your productivity throughout the day.

Improves time estimation: The Pomodoro Technique helps you develop a better understanding of the time required for different tasks. As you track the number of Pomodoros it takes to complete certain activities you can make more accurate time estimations and plan your schedule accordingly.

Motivates and rewards progress: Completing a Pomodoro and taking a short break acts as a mini-reward system. This sense of achievement and progress motivates you to continue working and complete more Pomodoros.

3.5 Scheduling Regular Breaks

Scheduling regular breaks is crucial for maintaining productivity preventing burnout and improving overall well-being. Working for long periods without breaks can lead to diminished focus decreased motivation and increased stress levels. By incorporating regular breaks into your daily routine you can recharge your energy improve mental clarity and sustain productivity.

Here are some key benefits of scheduling regular breaks:

Rest and rejuvenation: Breaks provide an opportunity to rest and recharge both physically and mentally. Stepping away from work allows your brain to relax and recover reducing fatigue and increasing your ability to concentrate when you return.

Improved creativity and problem-solving: Taking breaks allows your subconscious mind to work on problems in the background. It stimulates creativity enhances problem-solving abilities and leads to fresh insights and ideas.

Increased productivity: Regular breaks can actually boost productivity rather than hinder it. By stepping away from your work periodically you prevent productivity slumps maintain focus and approach tasks with renewed energy and clarity.

Enhanced overall well-being: Taking breaks supports overall mental and physical well-being. It reduces stress and allows you to engage in activities that promote relaxation such as walking stretching or meditation. Regular breaks also help prevent musculoskeletal issues associated with prolonged sitting or repetitive tasks.

How to schedule regular breaks effectively:

Short breaks: Schedule short breaks of 5 to 10 minutes every hour or two while working on a task. Use this time to stretch walk around grab a healthy snack or engage in a quick mindfulness exercise.

Longer breaks: Incorporate longer breaks of 15 to 30 minutes after completing a few hours of focused work. During these breaks engage in activities that help you relax and recharge such as taking a walk listening to music practicing deep breathing or doing something enjoyable.

Plan enjoyable activities: Use your breaks to engage in activities that you find enjoyable or fulfilling. This could include reading listening to a podcast playing an instrument or spending time with loved ones. Engaging in activities that bring you joy helps reduce stress and rejuvenate your mind.

By incorporating regular breaks into your schedule you can improve your overall well-being maintain productivity and avoid burnout.

In summary effective time management is crucial for maximizing productivity and achieving your goals. By identifying and minimizing time wasters implementing time blocking techniques breaking tasks into manageable chunks utilizing the Pomodoro Technique and scheduling regular breaks you can significantly improve your time management skills. Remember that time management is a skill that requires practice and adaptation to your own preferences and work style. Experiment with different strategies and techniques to find what works best for you. With consistent effort and conscious attention to your time you can master the art of effective time management.

Chapter 4: Improving Focus and Concentration

Improving focus and concentration is essential for enhancing productivity and achieving better results in various aspects of life. It involves adopting strategies to minimize distractions and stay engaged in tasks. Techniques such as setting specific goals, creating a conducive work environment, and practicing mindfulness can aid in sharpening concentration. Additionally, managing time effectively, taking regular breaks, and prioritizing tasks can help maintain sustained attention. Developing these skills is crucial for success in work and study, as it enables individuals to complete tasks more efficiently and with higher quality outcomes. Improving focus and concentration is an ongoing process that can lead to increased productivity, reduced errors, and a greater sense of accomplishment.

4.1 Creating a Distraction-Free Environment

Creating a distraction-free environment is crucial for improving focus and concentration. External distractions can greatly hinder our ability to stay focused on the task at hand. Here are some strategies you can implement to create an environment conducive to deep work:

1. Minimize physical distractions: Remove any unnecessary items from your workspace that may divert your attention. Keep your desk clean and organized to reduce visual clutter.

2. Noise control: Reduce ambient noise by finding a quiet space or using noise-cancelling headphones. If complete silence hampers your productivity you can try background music or white noise to help you concentrate.

3. Digital distractions: Turn off notifications on your devices or use apps that block certain websites or apps during focused work sessions. Managing your digital environment can significantly decrease the temptation to check social media or respond to non-urgent messages.

4. Designate a dedicated workspace: Having a specific area solely for work can help create a mental boundary between work and personal life. This separation can enhance focus and concentration.

Example 1: Sarah is a freelance writer who struggled with distractions while working from home. She decided to convert a spare room into a home office complete with a desk ergonomic chair and minimal decor. By creating a designated workspace Sarah was able to separate work from leisure activities resulting in improved focus and productivity.

Example 2: John a software developer was easily distracted by the noise of construction outside his apartment. To combat this he invested in noise-cancelling headphones. By blocking out the external distractions John found himself able to concentrate better on his coding tasks and complete them more efficiently.

4.2 Practicing Mindfulness and Meditation

Mindfulness and meditation are powerful techniques for improving focus and concentration. They involve training the mind to stay present and aware of the current moment without judgment. Regular practice of mindfulness and meditation can help cultivate a clear and calm mental state allowing for greater focus and attention on tasks.

1. Mindful breathing: Take a few minutes each day to focus on your breath. Pay attention to the sensation of the breath entering and leaving your body. Whenever your mind starts to wander gently bring your attention back to the breath.

2. Body scan meditation: Lie down or sit comfortably and scan your body from head to toe paying attention to any sensations or areas of tension. This practice helps bring awareness to the present moment and increases bodily relaxation.

3. Mindful eating: Slow down and savor each bite of your meals. Pay attention to the flavors textures and smells of the food. This practice increases awareness and reduces mindless eating leading to improved focus and digestion.

4. Meditation apps: Various smartphone apps such as Headspace Calm and Insight Timer offer guided meditation sessions tailored to different needs and time constraints. These apps can be helpful for beginners or those looking for structure in their meditation practice.

Example 3: Lisa a marketing manager often felt overwhelmed and scattered during work. She started to incorporate a short meditation session into her morning routine. By taking just 10 minutes to sit quietly and focus on her breath Lisa found that her mind felt clearer and more focused throughout the day allowing her to tackle tasks with greater efficiency.

Example 4: Tom a college student struggled with maintaining concentration while studying for his exams. He started using a mindfulness technique called "Pomodoro Technique where he would study intensely for 25 minutes followed by a 5-minute break. During these breaks he would practice mindful breathing or quick meditation which helped him recharge and stay focused for the next study session.

4.3 Utilizing Time-Blocking for Deep Work Sessions

Time-blocking is a powerful productivity technique that involves scheduling specific blocks of time for focused work. By allocating dedicated time slots for particular tasks you create a structured working schedule that minimizes distractions and optimizes productivity.

1. Identify priorities: Determine the most important tasks that you need to accomplish. Prioritize them based on urgency and importance and allocate specific time blocks for each task accordingly.

2. Set achievable goals: Break down larger tasks into smaller manageable chunks. Assign realistic time frames for completing these smaller tasks and allocate specific time blocks to work on

them.

3. Single-tasking: During your time blocks for deep work focus solely on the task at hand. Avoid multitasking as it divides your attention and reduces the quality of your work.

4. Take breaks: It's essential to schedule short breaks between blocks of focused work. Use these breaks to stretch move around or engage in brief relaxation techniques. This allows your mind to reset and maintain productivity for more extended periods.

Example 5: James a project manager found it challenging to balance his managerial duties and focus on his individual work tasks. He started using time-blocking to allocate dedicated blocks of time for responding to emails attending meetings and working on project deliverables. By setting aside specific time slots for deep work James was able to improve his productivity and ensure dedicated focus on important tasks.

Example 6: Maria a freelance graphic designer struggled with procrastination and finding motivation to start her creative projects. She began time-blocking her day allocating focused work blocks for designing brainstorming and researching inspiration. This structured approach helped Maria eliminate distractions overcome procrastination and increase her creative output.

4.4 Setting Clear Boundaries and Communicating Effectively

Setting clear boundaries and communicating effectively with others is crucial for maintaining focus and concentration. By clearly expressing your needs and limitations you can minimize interruptions and create an environment that supports your productivity.

1. Establish communication guidelines: Communicate with your colleagues family members or roommates about your need for uninterrupted work time. Set expectations regarding when you can be approached and when it's necessary to limit distractions.

2. Use visual cues: When you are in a focused work state use visual cues to indicate that you should not be disturbed such as closing your office door wearing headphones or displaying a "Do Not Disturb" sign.

3. Prioritize tasks: Be clear about your priorities and communicate them appropriately to team members or clients. This helps manage expectations and ensures that you have adequate time and space to work on critical tasks.

4. Learn to say no: Practice setting boundaries by politely declining requests or invitations that do not align with your current priorities. Learning to say no helps protect your time and energy for essential tasks.

Example 7: Mark a software engineer often faced interruptions from colleagues seeking assistance while he was deep in concentration. He implemented a visual cue system where he wore a red hat during focused work sessions to indicate that he should not be disturbed unless it was urgent. This practice helped his colleagues recognize when he needed uninterrupted time reducing non-essential interruptions.

Example 8: Rachel a teacher struggled with constantly receiving non-urgent messages from parents during her work hours. She communicated her boundaries by setting specific office hours for parent communication and politely informing them of her availability. By setting clear expectations Rachel was able to maintain her focus during teaching hours and address parent concerns during the designated office hours.

In conclusion improving focus and concentration requires creating a distraction-free environment practicing mindfulness utilizing time-blocking and setting clear boundaries. By implementing these strategies and techniques you can enhance your ability to stay focused and achieve greater productivity in various areas of your life.

Chapter 5: Enhancing Decision-Making Skills

Enhancing decision-making skills is vital for making informed choices in both personal and professional life. It involves developing a structured approach to evaluate options, assess risks, and consider consequences. Techniques such as gathering relevant information, setting clear objectives, and involving critical thinking can aid in making better decisions. Moreover, seeking advice or feedback from others can provide valuable insights. Decision-making skills also benefit from practicing self-awareness and emotional intelligence to manage biases and emotions that might cloud judgment. By continually honing these skills, individuals can boost their confidence in decision-making, improve problem-solving abilities, and make choices that align with their long-term goals and values.

5.1 Gathering Sufficient Information:

One of the foundational aspects of effective decision-making is the ability to gather sufficient information. Making decisions based on limited or incomplete information can lead to poor outcomes. Therefore it is crucial to invest time and effort in gathering relevant and accurate information before making a decision.

For example let's consider a scenario where you are tasked with purchasing a new laptop for work. Before making a decision you would gather information about different laptop brands their features prices customer reviews and compatibility with your job requirements. By gathering sufficient information you can make an informed decision that aligns with your needs and preferences.

5.2 Analyzing Pros and Cons:

Once you have gathered sufficient information the next step is to analyze the pros and cons of the available options. By objectively evaluating the advantages and disadvantages you can gain a deeper understanding of the potential outcomes and make a more informed decision.

To illustrate imagine you are considering whether to accept a job offer at a new company. By analyzing the pros and cons you might discover that the new company offers a higher salary but it would require longer working hours and a longer commute. On the other hand your current job offers a more flexible schedule and a shorter commute but with a slightly lower salary. By weighing these pros and cons you can make a decision that considers the trade-offs and aligns with your priorities.

5.3 Considering Long-Term Implications:

In addition to analyzing the immediate pros and cons it is also crucial to consider the long-term implications of your decision. Some decisions may have immediate benefits but can lead to negative consequences in the future. It is essential to take a forward-thinking approach and consider the potential long-term impact before making a decision.

For instance let's consider the decision to start a new business. While the immediate excitement and potential for financial gain might be attractive it is crucial to consider the long-term implications. Factors such as market trends competition sustainability and scalability need to be evaluated to ensure that the decision aligns with your long-term goals and objectives.

5.4 Seeking Input from Others:

Another effective way to enhance decision-making skills is to seek input from others. Different perspectives can provide valuable insights and challenge your own biases or blind spots. By gathering diverse opinions you can make a more well-rounded and informed decision.

For example imagine you are trying to decide whether to invest in a particular stock. Instead of relying solely on your own analysis you might seek input from financial advisors experienced investors or even online forums where people discuss investment strategies. By considering a variety of opinions you can gain a broader perspective and make a more informed investment decision.

5.5 Making Timely Decisions:

While gathering information analyzing pros and cons and considering long-term implications are essential it is equally important to make timely decisions. Procrastination or indecisiveness can lead to missed opportunities or unnecessary delays in achieving your goals. Therefore developing the ability to make timely decisions is a crucial skill to enhance decision-making competence.

For instance let's say you have been contemplating whether to enroll in a professional development course that aligns with your career goals. You have gathered information analyzed the cost and benefits and considered the long-term implications. Making a timely decision rather than procrastinating can allow you to take advantage of the course and further develop your skills which can positively impact your career progression.

Conclusion:

Enhancing decision-making skills involves various strategies such as gathering sufficient information analyzing pros and cons considering long-term implications seeking input from others and making timely decisions. By incorporating these practices into your decision-making process you can make more informed effective and impactful decisions.

Remember decision-making is a skill that improves with practice and experience. Developing the ability to gather and analyze information consider long-term implications seek input from others and make timely decisions can help you become a more confident and efficient decision-maker.

Chapter 6: Effective Communication Techniques

Effective communication is essential in both personal and professional settings. It helps us convey our thoughts and ideas clearly understand others' perspectives build strong relationships and achieve our objectives. In this chapter we will explore various techniques that can enhance our communication skills and make us more effective communicators.

6.1 Active Listening and Asking Clarifying Questions

Active listening is a crucial skill in effective communication. It involves fully concentrating on and understanding the message being conveyed by the speaker. To be an active listener you need to focus your attention on the speaker avoid distractions and give them your undivided attention.

One way to show active listening is through non-verbal cues such as maintaining eye contact nodding your head and using appropriate facial expressions. These gestures indicate that you are engaged and interested in what the speaker is saying.

Another important aspect of active listening is asking clarifying questions. Sometimes the speaker's message may not be clear or may be open to interpretation. By asking questions you can seek clarification and ensure that you understand the message accurately. This also demonstrates your interest in the conversation and encourages the speaker to elaborate and provide more information.

For example imagine you are in a team meeting where a colleague presents a new project proposal. Instead of passively listening you engage in active listening by maintaining eye contact nodding and asking questions to clarify certain aspects of the proposal. This helps you gain a deeper understanding of the project and enables you to provide valuable input.

6.2 Setting Clear Objectives and Expectations

Clear communication starts with setting clear objectives and expectations. When communicating it is important to define the purpose and desired outcome of the conversation. This helps both parties understand the primary focus and align their efforts towards achieving the intended goals.

For instance in a work project you should clearly communicate the project objectives milestones and deadlines to your team members. By doing so you provide them with a clear understanding of what needs to be accomplished and by when. This clarity enables effective collaboration and ensures that everyone is working towards the same end goal.

Setting expectations is equally important. Communicating what you expect from others in terms of quality timeliness or any other relevant factor sets the standard for performance. This reduces misunderstandings and enables everyone to meet the desired outcomes.

For example suppose you are working with a freelance designer to create a logo for your business. Clearly communicating your expectations regarding the design style color palette and desired deliverables ensures that the designer knows what is expected and can deliver accordingly.

6.3 Utilizing Communication Tools and Technologies

Advancements in technology have greatly influenced the way we communicate. There are now numerous tools and technologies available that can enhance our communication efficiency and effectiveness.

Email instant messaging video conferencing and project management software are just a few examples of communication tools that can streamline communication processes and improve collaboration. These tools enable quick and efficient communication regardless of geographical barriers. They also allow for easy sharing of documents feedback and updates.

For instance if you are collaborating on a project with team members from different locations utilizing video conferencing software can facilitate virtual meetings enabling face-to-face communication and providing a platform for discussions and decision-making. It saves time and travel expenses while still allowing effective communication.

However it is important to choose the right tool for the purpose. Not all communication tools are suitable for every situation. Assessing the specific requirements of your communication and selecting the appropriate tool can significantly enhance your effectiveness in conveying your message.

6.4 Providing Constructive Feedback

Constructive feedback plays a vital role in effective communication. It helps individuals improve their performance provides guidance and encourages growth. When providing feedback it is important to be specific objective and constructive.

Being specific means providing feedback on the specific actions behaviors or outcomes you want to address. Vague or general feedback can leave the receiver confused and unsure of what needs to be improved. By being specific you provide clarity and direction for improvement.

Objectivity is crucial when providing feedback. It entails focusing on facts rather than personal opinions or emotions. Objective feedback is more likely to be received well and less likely to create defensiveness or conflict.

Constructive feedback should also be balanced with positive aspects. Acknowledging strengths and highlighting areas of improvement creates a more supportive and encouraging environment for growth.

For example when providing feedback to a team member on their presentation skills instead of saying "Your presentation was horrible provide specific and objective feedback like "Your voice projection was low and you could try using more visuals to enhance the audience's understanding. However your content was well-researched and your examples were effective."

6.5 Building Strong Relationships

Strong relationships are based on effective communication. Building relationships requires active listening empathy and understanding. It involves creating an environment where individuals feel valued respected and heard.

To build strong relationships it is important to invest time in personal interactions. Taking the time to get to know people on a personal level can strengthen rapport foster trust and create a sense of camaraderie. This can be as simple as engaging in small talk asking about their interests or showing genuine care and concern.

Empathy is also a crucial component of building strong relationships. By putting yourself in others' shoes and trying to understand their perspectives and emotions you demonstrate empathy. This helps create a connection and fosters mutual understanding.

For example if a team member is dealing with a personal issue that affects their performance showing empathy by offering support flexibility or resources can strengthen the relationship and build trust.

In conclusion effective communication techniques are essential for successful interactions and relationships. Active listening and asking clarifying questions enhance understanding while setting clear objectives and expectations ensure everyone is on the same page. Utilizing communication tools and technologies increases efficiency and providing constructive feedback promotes growth. Lastly building strong relationships requires active listening empathy and investing time in personal interactions. By honing these techniques we can become more effective communicators and achieve better outcomes in our personal and professional lives.

Chapter 7: Delegating and Outsourcing

Delegating and outsourcing are crucial strategies for effective workload management and achieving optimal efficiency. Delegating involves assigning tasks and responsibilities to others within a team, based on their skills and capabilities, to free up time for more critical activities. Outsourcing, on the other hand, involves contracting external professionals or organizations to handle specific tasks or functions, often to access specialized expertise.

These practices can help individuals and businesses streamline operations, reduce their workload, and focus on core competencies. Effective delegation requires clear communication, trust in team members, and regular follow-up. Outsourcing demands careful vendor selection and management to ensure desired results.

By mastering these skills, individuals and organizations can optimize resource allocation, improve productivity, and concentrate on strategic priorities, ultimately leading to better outcomes and growth.

7.1 Identifying Tasks Suitable for Delegation:

Delegation is the process of assigning tasks and responsibilities to others allowing them to take on more responsibility and authority. However not all tasks are suitable for delegation. It is important to identify tasks that can be delegated effectively. Here are a few factors to consider when identifying tasks suitable for delegation:

1. Routine tasks: Tasks that are repetitive and do not require specific knowledge or expertise are ideal for delegation. For example data entry filing or scheduling appointments can be easily delegated.

2. Time-consuming tasks: Tasks that take up a significant amount of time but are not critical for your role can be delegated. This will free up your time for more strategic and high-priority tasks. For instance organizing meetings conducting research or preparing reports can be delegated.

3. Tasks that align with the skills and capabilities of others: Look for tasks that match the skills and abilities of your team members. Assign tasks that play to their strengths and help them grow in their roles. For example if you have a team member who excels in graphic design you can delegate the task of creating visual content for marketing materials.

4. Tasks that promote development: Delegation can also be used as a tool for employee development. Assigning tasks that challenge your team members and allow them to learn new skills can help enhance their professional growth. For instance delegating a project management task to someone who is eager to develop their leadership skills.

Example:

Let's say you are a marketing manager in a company. You have been assigned the task of organizing a company event which includes selecting a venue coordinating with vendors managing the budget and creating promotional materials. Instead of handling all these tasks yourself you can delegate specific responsibilities to your team members. You can assign one person to research and select a suitable venue another person to coordinate with vendors someone else to manage the budget and another team member to handle the creation of promotional materials. By delegating these tasks you can focus on overseeing the entire event and ensuring its success.

7.2 Selecting the Right People for Delegation:

Once you have identified tasks suitable for delegation the next step is to select the right people to delegate those tasks to. Effective delegation requires careful consideration of individuals' skills capabilities and experience. Here are some factors to consider when selecting the right people for delegation:

1. Skills and expertise: Match the required skills and expertise for the task with the capabilities of potential delegates. Look for individuals who have the necessary knowledge and experience to handle the task effectively. For example if you need to delegate a technical task you would choose someone with a strong technical background.

2. Motivation and interest: Consider the motivation and interest of potential delegates. Find individuals who are enthusiastic about taking on new responsibilities and are eager to learn and grow. Ensure that the task aligns with their interests and

aspirations.

3. Availability and workload: Assess the availability and workload of potential delegates. Make sure they have the time and capacity to take on additional responsibilities. Avoid overburdening individuals who are already struggling to meet their existing commitments.

4. Development opportunities: Delegation can serve as a tool for employee development. Consider individuals who would benefit from the task in terms of skill enhancement and professional growth. Assigning tasks that stretch their capabilities can boost their confidence and competence.

Example:

Let's continue with the example of organizing a company event. You have identified specific tasks suitable for delegation such as venue selection vendor coordination budget management and promotional material creation. To select the right people for delegation you would assess the skills and interests of your team members. You may assign the venue selection task to someone with experience in event planning or location scouting. The vendor coordination task can be delegated to another team member who has proven negotiation and communication skills. The budget management task can be assigned to someone with financial expertise and the promotional materials task can be given to a team member with strong design skills. By selecting individuals based on their capabilities and interests you increase the chances of successful delegation.

7.3 Clear Instructions and Expectations:

When delegating tasks it is crucial to provide clear instructions and set expectations with the individuals taking on the responsibilities. Clear communication ensures that everyone is on the same page and understands what needs to be done. Here are some guidelines for providing clear instructions and expectations:

1. Clearly define the task: Clearly explain the task to the delegate including the purpose desired outcome and any specific requirements. Provide as much detail as necessary but avoid overwhelming them with unnecessary information.

2. Set clear goals and objectives: Clearly state the goals and objectives that need to be achieved. Establish measurable targets to assess progress and success. For example if delegating a marketing project you may set goals such as increasing website traffic by 20% or generating 100 new leads.

3. Discuss deadlines and timelines: Clearly communicate the deadlines and timeline for completion of the task. Make sure there is a shared understanding of when each stage or milestone needs to be achieved. Set realistic deadlines to avoid undue pressure or rushed work.

4. Provide necessary resources and support: Identify and provide the resources and support required to complete the task successfully. This may include access to tools information training or collaboration with other team members. Ensure that the delegate knows where to find these resources and how to seek support if needed.

Example:

In the case of delegating the task of organizing a company event you would provide clear instructions and expectations to each of the delegates. For the venue selection task you would clearly define the criteria for selecting a suitable venue such as capacity location and amenities. You would discuss the budget and any restrictions to be considered. You would also set a deadline for presenting options and a timeline for finalizing the venue. Similarly for other delegated tasks you would provide specific instructions discuss desired outcomes set deadlines and offer necessary resources and support. This clear communication ensures that everyone understands their role and responsibilities reducing the chances of misunderstandings or errors.

7.4 Monitoring Progress and Providing Support:

Effective delegation involves monitoring the progress of delegated tasks to ensure they are on track and providing support when needed. Regular monitoring enables you to identify potential issues early and take corrective action. Here are some key steps for monitoring progress and providing support:

1. Regular check-ins: Schedule regular check-in meetings or status updates to review progress. Use these opportunities to assess the delegate's understanding of the task clarify any questions or concerns and provide feedback.

2. Track milestones and deadlines: Keep track of milestones and deadlines to ensure that progress is being made on time. This can be done through project management tools shared calendars

or regular updates from the delegate.

3. Offer guidance and support: Be available to offer guidance and support as needed. This may involve answering questions providing advice or sharing resources. Encourage open communication and create a supportive environment for the delegate to seek help when required.

4. Provide constructive feedback: Regularly provide feedback on the delegate's performance. Recognize their accomplishments and provide constructive criticism to help them improve. Offer specific feedback on what was done well and areas for improvement.

Example:

Continuing with the example of organizing a company event you would monitor the progress of each delegated task by scheduling regular check-ins. During these meetings you would review the delegate's progress and provide support and guidance where necessary. For instance if the delegate responsible for vendor coordination encounters challenges in negotiating favorable terms you can offer advice on negotiation techniques or connect them with someone experienced in vendor management. By proactively monitoring progress and providing support you ensure that the delegated tasks stay on track and the delegates feel supported in their responsibilities.

7.5 Evaluating Results and Providing Feedback:

Once delegated tasks have been completed it is essential to evaluate the results and provide feedback to the individuals involved. Evaluation helps assess the effectiveness of delegation and identify areas for improvement. Here are some steps for evaluating results and providing feedback:

1. Assess outcomes: Assess whether the desired outcomes and objectives have been achieved. Evaluate the quality of the work adherence to instructions and overall success of the task. Compare the actual results with the goals set during delegation.

2. Provide feedback: Provide timely feedback to the individuals involved. Recognize their accomplishments and acknowledge their efforts. Offer specific feedback on what was done well and areas that could be improved. Ensure that feedback is constructive and focused on learning and growth.

3. Address any issues or errors: If any issues or errors were encountered during the delegated tasks address them with the individuals involved. Determine the root causes of the issues and identify corrective actions or solutions to prevent similar problems in the future.

4. Document lessons learned: Document lessons learned from the delegation process. Capture insights into what worked well what could be improved and any adjustments to be made for future delegation. This documentation can serve as a reference for refining delegation processes and practices.

Example:

In the case of organizing a company event once all delegated tasks are completed you would evaluate the outcomes. Assess whether the event was successful in meeting its objectives such as attendee satisfaction staying within budget and achieving the desired event atmosphere. Provide feedback to the individuals involved in each delegated task recognizing their contributions and offering suggestions for improvement. For example if the promotional materials did not have the desired impact provide feedback on areas for improvement such as design messaging or the choice of marketing channels. Document any lessons learned such as refining the selection criteria for vendors or providing more comprehensive guidelines for future event planning. By evaluating results and providing feedback you can continuously improve the effectiveness of delegation.

In conclusion effective delegation involves identifying tasks suitable for delegation selecting the right people for delegation providing clear instructions and expectations monitoring progress and providing support and evaluating results and providing feedback. By following these steps you can successfully delegate tasks empower your team members and achieve greater productivity and efficiency in your work. Delegation is a valuable skill for leaders and managers as it not only enables you to focus on more strategic tasks but also develops the capabilities and skills of your team members.

Chapter 8: Managing Energy and Well-being

Managing energy and well-being is essential for maintaining optimal performance and overall quality of life. It involves strategies to sustain physical, mental, and emotional vitality. Techniques such as regular exercise, balanced nutrition, and adequate sleep contribute to physical well-being and increased energy levels.

Mental well-being benefits from mindfulness practices, stress management, and setting realistic expectations. Emotional well-being is nurtured through self-awareness, healthy relationships, and emotional intelligence.

Balancing work and personal life, setting boundaries, and taking time for self-care are essential elements of managing energy and well-being. By prioritizing these aspects, individuals can enhance their resilience, reduce burnout, and maintain a high level of productivity and satisfaction in both personal and professional pursuits.

8.1 Prioritizing Self-Care Activities

Self-care is the practice of taking care of oneself in order to maintain and enhance one's physical mental and emotional well-being. It is crucial to prioritize self-care activities to ensure a balance between work personal life and overall well-being.

Self-care activities can vary from person to person as everyone has different needs and preferences. Some examples include:

1. Engaging in hobbies: Hobbies provide an outlet for relaxation and creativity. Whether it's painting playing a musical instrument gardening or cooking engaging in activities that bring joy and fulfillment can greatly enhance well-being.

2. Practicing mindfulness and meditation: Mindfulness and meditation are techniques that help promote mental clarity reduce stress and improve overall well-being. By focusing attention on the present moment individuals can cultivate a sense of calm and relaxation.

3. Spending time with loved ones: Nurturing relationships is an essential part of self-care. Spending quality time with family and friends helps to strengthen social connections provide emotional support and reduce stress.

4. Practicing self-reflection and journaling: Self-reflection allows individuals to gain insight into their thoughts feelings and behaviors. Journaling provides a space for self-expression and can help alleviate stress and anxiety by processing emotions and experiences.

5. Engaging in physical activity: Regular exercise is not only

beneficial for physical health but also has a positive impact on mental well-being. Engaging in activities such as jogging dancing yoga or team sports can boost mood reduce stress and improve overall energy levels.

The key is to identify self-care activities that resonate with you and make them a priority in your daily or weekly routine. By fitting self-care into your schedule you can enhance your overall well-being and manage your energy effectively.

8.2 Establishing Healthy Habits

Establishing healthy habits is essential for maintaining energy levels and overall well-being. Healthy habits are behaviors that contribute to physical mental and emotional well-being and are sustained over time. Here are some examples of healthy habits:

1. Eating a balanced diet: Consuming a variety of nutrient-dense foods provides the body with essential vitamins minerals and energy. A balanced diet includes whole grains lean proteins fruits and vegetables and healthy fats.

2. Staying hydrated: Hydration is vital for maintaining energy and overall health. Drinking an adequate amount of water each day helps regulate body temperature support digestion and promote cognitive function.

3. Practicing stress management techniques: Chronic stress can negatively impact well-being and energy levels. Adopting stress management techniques such as deep breathing relaxation exercises or engaging in hobbies can help reduce stress and

boost overall well-being.

4. Limiting screen time: Excessive screen time especially before bed can disrupt sleep patterns and impact overall well-being. Establishing limits on screen usage such as turning off screens an hour before bedtime can improve sleep quality and energy levels.

5. Taking regular breaks: Taking short breaks throughout the day can help prevent mental and physical fatigue. Engaging in activities or practices such as stretching walking or mindfulness exercises during breaks can renew energy and improve focus.

Establishing healthy habits requires consistency and commitment. By integrating these habits into your daily routine you can optimize your energy levels enhance well-being and experience greater overall productivity.

8.3 Getting Adequate Sleep and Rest

Adequate sleep and rest are essential for maintaining energy levels cognitive function and overall well-being. Lack of sleep can lead to fatigue decreased focus and increased stress levels. Here are some strategies to promote quality sleep and rest:

1. Establishing a sleep routine: Going to bed and waking up at the same time each day helps regulate the body's internal clock and enhances sleep quality. Creating a bedtime routine that includes wind-down activities such as reading or taking a warm bath signals the body to prepare for sleep.

2. Creating a sleep-friendly environment: Creating a comfortable and relaxing sleep environment can promote restful sleep. Ensure your bedroom is cool dark and quiet and invest in a supportive mattress and pillows that suit your preferences.

3. Limiting exposure to stimulating activities before bed: Engaging in stimulating activities such as watching TV using electronic devices or consuming caffeine close to bedtime can interfere with sleep. It is advisable to limit these activities at least an hour before bed.

4. Practicing relaxation techniques: Engaging in relaxation techniques such as deep breathing exercises guided meditation or progressive muscle relaxation can help calm the mind and prepare the body for sleep.

5. Taking regular breaks and downtime: Resting and recharging throughout the day is crucial for maintaining energy levels. Taking short breaks disconnecting from work-related activities and engaging in enjoyable leisure activities can help prevent burnout and promote overall well-being.

Getting adequate sleep and rest should be a priority to optimize energy levels cognitive function and overall well-being. By implementing these strategies individuals can establish healthy sleep patterns and enhance their overall quality of life.

8.4 Nurturing Physical Fitness

Physical fitness is an integral component of overall well-being. Engaging in regular physical activity not only improves physical health but also has positive effects on mental health cognitive function and energy levels. Here are some examples of physical fitness activities:

1. Cardiovascular exercise: Activities such as jogging cycling swimming or dancing elevate heart rate improve cardiovascular health and boost overall endurance. Regular cardiovascular exercise enhances energy levels and promotes a sense of well-being.

2. Strength training: Engaging in strength training exercises such as weightlifting or bodyweight exercises helps build and maintain muscle strength and endurance. Strength training improves overall physical fitness metabolic function and energy levels.

3. Flexibility exercises: Activities such as yoga or Pilates enhance flexibility balance and body awareness. These exercises help prevent injury improve posture and promote relaxation.

4. Outdoor activities: Engaging in outdoor activities such as hiking gardening or playing sports not only provides physical exercise but also allows individuals to connect with nature reduce stress levels and improve well-being.

The key to nurturing physical fitness is to find activities that are enjoyable and align with personal preferences and goals. Regular physical activity not only improves physical health but also boosts energy levels reduces stress and enhances overall well-being.

8.5 Reducing Stress and Practicing Work-Life Balance

Stress is a common aspect of daily life and can significantly impact overall well-being and energy levels. Practicing stress reduction techniques and establishing a healthy work-life balance can help manage stress effectively. Here are some strategies to reduce stress and achieve work-life balance:

1. Prioritizing and setting boundaries: Identify your priorities and set boundaries to protect your time and energy. Learn to say no to unnecessary commitments and delegate tasks when possible. Setting limits ensures that you have time for self-care relaxation and activities that bring you joy.

2. Time management: Effective time management techniques such as creating schedules setting realistic goals and prioritizing tasks can reduce stress and enhance productivity. Learning to manage time effectively allows for a better balance between work and personal life.

3. Engaging in relaxation techniques: Practicing relaxation techniques such as deep breathing meditation or mindfulness exercises can help reduce stress levels and promote a sense of calm. Incorporating these activities into your daily routine can improve overall well-being and energy levels.

4. Building a support system: Cultivating a support system of family friends or colleagues can provide emotional support guidance and help in managing stress. Sharing concerns and seeking advice from trusted individuals can alleviate stress and provide different perspectives.

5. Taking regular breaks and vacations: Allocating regular breaks throughout the day and planning vacations can help recharge and reduce stress levels. Stepping away from work-related activities allows time for relaxation leisure activities and a break from daily stressors.

By implementing these strategies individuals can effectively manage stress and achieve a healthy work-life balance. Prioritizing self-care setting boundaries and incorporating relaxation techniques into daily routines can enhance overall well-being energy levels and productivity.

In conclusion managing energy and well-being is essential for maintaining overall health productivity and happiness. Prioritizing self-care activities establishing healthy habits getting adequate sleep and rest nurturing physical fitness reducing stress and practicing work-life balance are essential components of managing energy and well-being. By implementing these strategies and making them a priority individuals can optimize their energy levels promote well-being and lead a fulfilling and balanced life.

100 productive Tips

Time Management and Planning:

1. Prioritize tasks using the Eisenhower Matrix (urgent vs. important).
2. Create a to-do list for each day.
3. Use time-blocking to schedule your day.
4. Set SMART goals (Specific, Measurable, Achievable, Relevant, Time-bound).
5. Plan your week on Sunday or the night before.
6. Use productivity apps like Todoist, Trello, or Asana to organize tasks.
7. Limit multitasking; focus on one task at a time.
8. Use the Pomodoro Technique (25 minutes work, 5 minutes break).
9. Batch similar tasks to avoid switching contexts frequently.
10. Learn to say no to tasks that don't align with your goals.

Workspace and Environment:

11. Create a clutter-free and organized workspace.
12. Use a comfortable chair and ergonomic desk setup.
13. Ensure good lighting to reduce eye strain.
14. Keep essential supplies within arm's reach.

15. Use noise-canceling headphones in a noisy environment.
16. Decorate your workspace with motivational items.
17. Keep your workspace clean and tidy.
18. Minimize distractions by decluttering your desk.
19. Set up a dedicated workspace to separate work from leisure.
20. Invest in technology that enhances productivity (e.g., dual monitors).

Task Management:

21. Break tasks into smaller, manageable steps.
22. Use the 2-minute rule for quick tasks (if it takes less than 2 minutes, do it now).
23. Delegate tasks when possible.
24. Use the "Eat That Frog" principle - tackle the most challenging task first.
25. Review your task list regularly to stay on track.
26. Use task management apps to track progress.
27. Keep a notebook or digital note-taking app for ideas and tasks.
28. Set deadlines for tasks to create a sense of urgency.
29. Use the "Two-Minute Rule" for quick decisions (if a decision takes less than two minutes, make it immediately).
30. Use the "3 Most Important Tasks" method to identify daily priorities.

Time Saving:

31. Automate repetitive tasks using tools like Zapier.
32. Use keyboard shortcuts for common actions.
33. Delegate or outsource tasks that aren't your strengths.
34. Use text expansion tools to save typing time.
35. Limit social media and email checking to specific times.

36. Unsubscribe from email newsletters and notifications.
37. Use templates for common emails and documents.
38. Use the "Snooze" feature in email to manage incoming messages.
39. Batch process email and social media.
40. Set up filters and labels to organize your inbox.

Focus and Concentration:

41. Practice mindfulness meditation to improve focus.
42. Minimize notifications on your devices.
43. Put your phone in Do Not Disturb mode during work hours.
44. Use website blockers to limit access to distracting sites.
45. Create a dedicated music playlist for work.
46. Use white noise or nature sounds to drown out distractions.
47. Prioritize deep work sessions for important tasks.
48. Take short breaks to recharge and avoid burnout.
49. Use the 2-hour rule (work for 2 hours, then take a longer break).
50. Practice the "10-3-2-1-0" rule for better sleep: 10 hours before bed, stop consuming caffeine; 3 hours, stop eating; 2 hours, stop working; 1 hour, stop screen time; 0, go to sleep.

Self-Care and Health:

51. Get enough sleep (7-9 hours per night).
52. Exercise regularly to boost energy and focus.
53. Eat a balanced diet to fuel your brain and body.
54. Stay hydrated by drinking enough water throughout the day.
55. Take short walks to refresh your mind.
56. Practice deep breathing exercises for stress relief.

57. Avoid overworking and take regular breaks.
58. Maintain a work-life balance to prevent burnout.
59. Schedule downtime for hobbies and relaxation.
60. Get regular check-ups and prioritize your health.

Learning and Personal Growth:

61. Read books, articles, and research to expand your knowledge.
62. Set aside time for continuous learning and skill development.
63. Attend workshops, seminars, and webinars.
64. Seek feedback to improve your skills and work.
65. Join professional networks and associations.
66. Create a personal development plan.
67. Keep a journal to reflect on your progress and goals.
68. Surround yourself with positive and supportive people.
69. Stay curious and open-minded.
70. Embrace failure as a learning opportunity.

Technology and Tools:

71. Use project management software to collaborate efficiently.
72. Invest in a high-quality laptop or computer.
73. Learn keyboard shortcuts for your most-used software.
74. Use cloud storage for easy access to documents.
75. Regularly update your software and apps.
76. Back up your data regularly.
77. Use password management tools to secure accounts.
78. Learn to troubleshoot basic tech issues.
79. Customize your device settings for productivity.
80. Use a second monitor to increase screen real estate.

Communication and Collaboration:

81. Schedule regular team meetings to stay aligned.
82. Use video conferencing for face-to-face communication.
83. Practice active listening in meetings and conversations.
84. Set clear expectations for team members.
85. Use collaboration tools like Slack and Microsoft Teams.
86. Develop effective email communication skills.
87. Provide constructive feedback to improve teamwork.
88. Use project management boards for visual progress tracking.
89. Encourage open and transparent communication.
90. Foster a positive and inclusive team culture.

Goal Setting and Motivation:

91. Visualize your goals and success regularly.
92. Celebrate small wins to stay motivated.
93. Break long-term goals into shorter milestones.
94. Share your goals with an accountability partner.
95. Create a vision board to inspire you.
96. Review and adjust your goals periodically.
97. Stay passionate about your work and purpose.
98. Find intrinsic motivation in your tasks.
99. Remind yourself why you want to be productive.
100. Stay persistent and don't give up on your goals.

100 Tips for success

Personal Development:

1. Believe in yourself and your abilities.
2. Set clear and achievable goals.
3. Continuously learn and seek new knowledge.
4. Embrace failure as a stepping stone to success.
5. Develop a growth mindset.
6. Practice self-discipline.
7. Cultivate a positive attitude.
8. Prioritize self-care and well-being.
9. Manage your time effectively.
10. Surround yourself with supportive people.

Career Success:

11. Network and build professional relationships.
12. Stay adaptable and open to change.
13. Seek feedback to improve your skills.
14. Take calculated risks.
15. Be proactive and take initiative.
16. Develop excellent communication skills.

17. Find a mentor or role model.
18. Stay organized and manage your tasks efficiently.
19. Continuously update your resume and LinkedIn profile.
20. Pursue opportunities for career growth.

Productivity and Time Management:

21. Set specific and measurable goals.
22. Prioritize tasks using the Eisenhower Matrix.
23. Use time-blocking to manage your schedule.
24. Avoid multitasking; focus on one task at a time.
25. Use the Pomodoro Technique for focused work.
26. Delegate tasks when possible.
27. Eliminate distractions from your workspace.
28. Learn to say no to non-essential commitments.
29. Use productivity tools and apps.
30. Take regular breaks to recharge.

Financial Success:

31. Create a budget and stick to it.
32. Save and invest wisely for the future.
33. Live below your means.
34. Pay off high-interest debt.
35. Diversify your income sources.
36. Learn about personal finance.
37. Avoid impulse purchases.
38. Plan for retirement early.
39. Set financial goals and milestones.
40. Be mindful of your spending habits.

Health and Well-being:

41. Exercise regularly to stay healthy.
42. Eat a balanced and nutritious diet.
43. Get enough sleep each night.
44. Practice stress management techniques.
45. Stay hydrated by drinking enough water.
46. Avoid excessive alcohol and tobacco use.
47. Schedule regular check-ups and screenings.
48. Prioritize mental health and seek support when needed.
49. Engage in hobbies and activities you enjoy.
50. Practice gratitude and mindfulness.

Relationships and Communication:

51. Listen actively in conversations.
52. Communicate your thoughts and feelings clearly.
53. Resolve conflicts through open dialogue.
54. Spend quality time with loved ones.
55. Show appreciation and express gratitude.
56. Apologize when you're wrong.
57. Practice empathy and understanding.
58. Surround yourself with positive influences.
59. Foster healthy boundaries in relationships.
60. Keep an open mind in interactions.

Education and Learning:

61. Read regularly to expand your knowledge.
62. Stay curious and ask questions.
63. Pursue continuous learning opportunities.

64. Set educational goals and milestones.
65. Seek feedback to improve your skills.
66. Stay informed about current events.
67. Attend workshops, seminars, and webinars.
68. Share your knowledge with others.
69. Challenge yourself to step out of your comfort zone.
70. Take notes and review what you learn.

Personal Growth and Happiness:

71. Practice gratitude daily.
72. Find joy in the little things.
73. Embrace change as a chance for growth.
74. Cultivate a sense of purpose.
75. Focus on what you can control.
76. Let go of negativity and toxic relationships.
77. Celebrate your successes, big and small.
78. Visualize your goals and aspirations.
79. Practice patience and resilience.
80. Take time for self-reflection.

Leadership and Influence:

81. Lead by example.
82. Inspire and motivate others.
83. Delegate tasks and responsibilities effectively.
84. Communicate a compelling vision.
85. Build trust and credibility.
86. Learn from great leaders and mentors.
87. Take ownership of your decisions.
88. Handle criticism with grace and humility.

89. Empower and uplift your team members.
90. Stay true to your values and principles.

Creativity and Innovation:

91. Embrace creativity as a problem-solving tool.
92. Seek inspiration from diverse sources.
93. Experiment with new ideas and approaches.
94. Encourage creativity in your workplace.
95. Collaborate with creative individuals.
96. Keep a journal for brainstorming and ideas.
97. Don't fear failure in creative endeavors.
98. Share your creative work with the world.
99. Stay open to feedback and refinement.
100. Believe in the power of your creativity.

9 788119 786756

Printed at Repro India Ltd.